BEST OLD FOLKS JOKES. EVER.

JOKES for SENIORS

CHANTELLE GRACE

BroadStreet
PUBLISHING

BroadStreet Publishing Group, LLC.
Savage, Minnesota, USA
Broadstreetpublishing.com

Best Old Folks Jokes Ever

978-1-4245-6290-9
978-1-4245-6291-6 (ebook)

Design by Chris Garborg | garborgdesign.com
Compiled and edited by Michelle Winger | literallyprecise.com

Printed in the United States of America.

21   22   23   24   25   26   27   7   6   5   4   3   2   1

CONTENTS

SIGNS OF THE TIMES

Two old guys, George and Pete, went to the movies.

A few minutes after it started, George heard Pete rustling around, searching on the floor under his seat.

"What are you doing?" asked George.

Pete, a little grumpy by this time, replied, "I had a caramel in my mouth, and it dropped out. I can't find it."

George said, "Forget it! It will be too dirty by now."

"I have to find it," said Pete. "My teeth are in it!"

Seeing her friend Patty wearing a new locket, Edith asks if there is a memento of some sort inside.

"Yes," says Patty, "a lock of my husband's hair."

"But Henry's still alive."

"I know, but his hair is gone."

I knew my husband's hearing had deteriorated after our friend who was new to the city asked where he could meet some singles.

"Well," said my husband, "I see them in the McDonalds parking lot diving for fries."

"Dear," I intervened, "he said singles... not seagulls."

An elderly man visited the doctor for a checkup.

"Mr. Smith, you're in great shape," said the doctor. "How do you do it?"

"Well," said Mr. Smith, "I don't drink, I don't smoke, and the good Lord looks out for me. For weeks now, every time I go to the bathroom in the middle of the night, he turns the light on for me."

Concerned, the doctor finds Mrs. Smith in the waiting room and tells her what her husband said.

"I don't think that's anything to worry about," she said. "And on the bright side, it does explain who's been peeing in the fridge."

An older gentleman was invited to his friends' home for dinner one evening. He was impressed by the way his buddy preceded every request to his wife with endearing terms like honey, my love, darling, sweetheart, pumpkin, etc. The couple had been married almost seventy years, and clearly, they were still very much in love.

While the wife was in the kitchen, the man leaned over and said to his host, "I think it's wonderful that after all these years, you still call your wife those endearing names."

The old man hung his head. "I have to tell you the truth," he said. "I forgot her name about ten years ago."

❖

I decided one day to reframe a favorite photograph of my mother and father from when they were dating.

After removing the picture from the frame, I turned it over, hoping to find a date. I didn't.

Instead, my mother had written "128 lbs."

The biggest loser at the weight-loss club was an elderly woman.

"How did you do it?" the others asked.

"Easy," she said. "Every night I take my teeth out at six o'clock."

An elderly gentleman in his mid-nineties, very well dressed with a flower in his lapel and smelling slightly of good aftershave, walked into an upscale restaurant and took a seat at the bar.

An elderly lady, mid-eighties, was seated there also.

The gentleman ordered a drink, took a sip, turned to the woman, and said, "So tell me, do I come here often?"

An elderly woman had just returned home after an evening at church, when she was startled by an intruder. As she caught the man in the act, she yelled, "Stop! Acts 2:38!" (Repent and be baptized, in the name of the Lord, so that your sins may be forgiven.)

The burglar stopped in his tracks.

The woman called the police and explained what had happened.

As the officer cuffed the man to take him in, he asked, "Why did you just stand there? All the lady did was yell a Scripture at you."

"Scripture?!" replied the burglar, "She said she had an AXE and TWO 38s!"

A church was holding a marriage seminar and the priest had asked Luigi, as his fiftieth wedding anniversary was approaching, to share some insight into how he managed to stay married to the same woman all those years.

Luigi said to the audience, "Well, I tried to treat her well and spend money on her. But the best thing I did was take her to Italy for our twentieth anniversary."

The priest said, "Luigi, you are an inspiration to all husbands here today. Please tell us what you plan to do for your wife for your fiftieth anniversary."

Luigi proudly replied, "I'm gonna go and get her."

"How was your blind date?"

"Terrible! He showed up in a 1932 Rolls-Royce."

"What's so terrible about that?"

"He was the original owner."

An elderly couple had dinner at another couple's house, and after eating, the wives left the table and went into the kitchen.

The two gentlemen were talking, and one said, "Last night we went out to a new restaurant and it was really great. I would recommend it very highly."

"What is the name of the restaurant?"

The man thought and thought and finally said, "What is the name of that flower you give someone you love? You know... the one that's red and has thorns?"

"Do you mean a rose?"

"Yes, that's the one." He then turned toward the kitchen and yelled, "Rose, what's the name of that restaurant we went to last night?"

I believe in loyalty.
When a woman reaches an age she likes, she should stick with it.

TECHNOLOGY

At age seventy, my grandfather bought his first riding lawn mower.

"This thing is great," he bragged to my brother. "It took me only an hour and a half to mow the lawn. It used to take your grandmother two days to do it all!"

Senior citizens have taken to texting with a new vigor.

They have even developed their own lingo.

ATD = At the Door

BFF = Best Friend Fell

BTW = Bring the Wheelchair

BYOT = Bring Your Own Teeth

CBM = Covered by Medicare

FWB = Friend with Beta-blockers

FWIW = Forgot Where I Was

GGPBL = Gotta Go Pacemaker Battery Low

GHA = Got Heartburn Again

LMDO = Laughing My Dentures Out

ROFLACGU = Rolling on Floor Laughing and Can't Get Up

TTYL = Talk to You Louder

Lincoln wanted to get his wife, Lucy, something nice for their fiftieth wedding anniversary, so he decided to buy her a cell phone. She was all excited; she loved her phone, and he explained all the features on it.

The next day, Lucy went shopping. Her phone rang, and it was Lincoln.

"Hi honey," he said. "How do you like your new phone?"

She replied, "I just love it. It's so small and your voice is clear as a bell. There's one thing I don't understand though."

"What's that?" asked Lincoln.

"How did you know I was at WalMart?"

❖

At a restaurant, a sign read "Karaoke Tonight!"

An older woman studied it before asking, "What kind of fish is that?"

Thanks to the cloud, all my devices are in sync.

It's only my brain that doesn't know what's going on.

Wife: I've been trying to call you all day.

Husband: With that?

Wife: Yes.

Husband: Sweetheart, that's a calculator.

A couple of elderly men were venting their frustrations about the woes of modern technology.

"I just can't ever seem to remember my darn passwords," grumbled one of them.

The other one smiled. "Oh really? I can never forget mine!"

"How do you manage it?" asked the first guy curiously.

"Well, I simply set all my passwords to *Incorrect* so that whenever I'm told that my password is incorrect, I'll remember it!"

The older gentleman called tech support to figure out a saved file issue. During the conversation, the IT tech asked if the man had backed up his hard drive. The old man replied, "I don't think so. How do I put it in reverse?"

BODY ACHES

The day after visiting a fair, my wife was in agony.

"You know you're past your prime," she said, "when you hurt all over and all you rode was the massage chair."

"Everything's starting to click for me!" said Grandpa at dinner.

"My knees, my elbows, my neck..."

The older you get...

the earlier it gets late.

❖

If my body were a car, I would trade
it in for a newer model. Every time I
cough, sneeze, or sputter, my radiator
leaks, and my exhaust backfires.

❖

Aging gracefully is the nice way of
saying...

you're slowly looking worse.

❖

A doctor says to his aging patient, "You have the body of a twenty-year-old, but you should return it. You're stretching it completely out of shape."

❖

I'm not aging like a fine wine.

I'm aging like a fine banana.

❖

When I went to get my flu shot, the young nurse told me she was very nervous as it was her first time.

I told her to give it her best shot.

❖

If God wanted us to touch our toes...

he would have put them on our knees.

At the age of sixty-five, my Grandma started walking five miles a day.

She's ninety-two now.

We have no idea where she is.

The only time the world beats a path to your door...

is when you're in the bathroom.

You get heavier as you get older because there's a lot more information in your head.

You're just really intelligent and your head couldn't hold any more, so you started filling up the rest of your body.

❖

Doctor: I think you have a severe iron deficiency.

Man: How do you know? I just walked in!

Doctor: Your clothes are all wrinkly.

❖

My Grandpa calls sixty minutes of pain an OWur.

❖

I fell asleep last night while reading old magazines.

I woke up this morning with back issues.

While discussing the severity of the flu for the elderly, my Grandpa asked if I had heard of the Amish flu.

He said you get a little buggy and hoarse.

Every time Grandma burns his grilled cheese sandwich, Grandpa gets a stomach ache.

He says he's black toast intolerant.

The older man moaned about his aching leg while training for a marathon.

"Don't worry about it," said a friend. "It will be worth it in the long run."

❖

My Grandma went into the doctor's office to ask about her sore stomach. The doctor just told her to quit her belly aching.

❖

Grandma hit her toe on the coffee table and was yelping in pain. As she hopped to the couch to sit down, Grandpa said, "Do you want me to call a toe truck?"

❖

I always know when my Irish grandfather has a stomach ache.

He'll be Dublin over.

❖

I had an appointment with two physicians. They told me the more pain I experience, the better I will feel.

What a strange pair-a-docs.

RETIREMENT

Retirement is the best thing that has happened to my grandpa.

"I never know what day of the week it is," he gloats. "All I know is, the day the big paper comes, I have to dress up and go to church."

When is a retiree's bedtime?

Three hours after he falls asleep on the couch.

How many retirees does it take to change a light bulb?

Only one, but it might take all day.

What's the biggest complaint of retirees?

There is not enough time to get everything done.

Why don't retirees mind being called Seniors?

The term comes with a ten percent discount.

Among retirees what is considered formal attire?

Tied shoes.

❖

Why do retirees count pennies?

They are the only ones who have the time.

❖

What is the common term for someone who enjoys work and refuses to retire?

Crazy.

❖

Why are retirees so slow to clean out the basement, attic, or garage?

They know as soon as they do, one of their adult kids will want to store stuff there.

What do retirees call a long lunch?

Normal.

What is the best way to describe retirement?

The never-ending coffee break.

What's the biggest advantage of going back to school as a retiree?

If you cut classes, no one calls your parents.

❖

The question isn't at what age you want to retire...

it's at what income.

❖

Golfers never retire,
they just lose their drive.

❖

Lumberjacks never retire,
they just pine away.

❖

Accountants don't retire,
they just lose their balance.

❖

Bank managers don't retire,
they just lose interest.

❖

Vehicle mechanics re-tire every day.

❖

Teachers don't retire,
they just mark time.

❖

Roofers don't retire,
they just wipe the slate clean.

❖

Engineers never retire,
they just lose their bearings.

❖

Beekeepers never retire,
they just buzz off.

❖

Musicians never retire,
they just decompose.

❖

Farmers never retire,
they just go to seed.

❖

Watchmakers never retire,
they just wind down.

❖

Academics never retire,
they just lose their faculties.

GENERATION GAP

The girl's class assignment was to interview an "old person" about his life, so she asked her uncle, "What was the biggest historical event that happened during your childhood?"

"I'd have to say the moonwalk," he replied.

She looked disappointed. "Really?" She asked. "That dance was so important to you?"

❖

My nine-year-old daughter walked in while I was getting ready for work.

"What are you doing?" she asked.

"Putting on my wrinkle cream," I answered.

"Oh," she said, walking away. "I thought they were natural."

The sight of my mother cleaning her dentures fascinated my young son. He sat riveted as she carefully took them out, brushed and rinsed them, and then popped them back in.

"Cool, Grandma!" he said. "Now take off your arm."

One of my fourth graders asked my teacher's assistant, "How old are you, Mrs. Glass?"

"You should never ask an adult's age," I broke in.

"That's okay," the assistant said smiling. "I'm fifty."

"Wow, you don't look that old," the boy said.

I was breathing a sigh of relief when another child chimed in, "Parts of her do."

❖

I asked my granddaughter if she wanted to watch the Grammy Awards.

She said, "I thought only old people could watch that."

❖

Hospital regulations require patients to be discharged in a wheelchair. A student nurse found an elderly gentleman already dressed and sitting on the bed with a suitcase at his feet. He insisted he didn't need the nurse's help to leave the hospital.

After a brief chat about rules being rules, the man reluctantly let the nurse wheel him to the elevator.

On the way down, she asked him if his wife was meeting him in the lobby.

"I don't know," he said. "She's still upstairs in the bathroom changing out of her hospital gown."

What did the young chicken say to the old one?

"You're no spring chicken!"

Our favorite museum in town displays quilts from around the country. When I visited recently, I asked the woman at the front desk about a senior discount. It wasn't to be.

"Ma'am," she said, "this is a quilt museum. We give discounts to teenagers."

What do you call a seventeen-year-old who stops aging?

Constantine.

I like having conversations with kids.

Grownups never ask me what my third favorite reptile is.

Dad: When I was your age, I ran a maratho.

Son: You mean marathon.

Dad: No, I didn't finish it.

Two young brothers were spending the night at their grandparents' home. When it was time for bed, the two boys knelt down and began to say their prayers.

Suddenly, the younger brother started yelling at the top of his voice, "I pray for a bicycle, and a new computer, and a trip to Disneyland!"

The older brother leaned over and whispered, "There's no need to shout. God isn't deaf."

"I know," said the younger brother, "but Grandma is!"

When I was a boy, I had a disease that required me to eat dirt three times a day in order to survive.

It's a good thing my older brother told me about it.

A teenage girl came across an elderly man sitting next to his radio, tapping his cane to a Lil Wayne song.

"Wow! I didn't think you'd like rap music!" she exclaimed.

"I didn't either," the old man replied. "It all started after my hip op."

I used to think my dad was really old.

He would say to me, "When I was your age, the Dead Sea was still alive!"

❖

Visiting my parents in their retirement village, I decided to go for a swim in the community pool while my father took a walk. I struck up a conversation with the only other person in the pool: a five-year-old boy.

After a while, my father returned from his walk and called out, "I'm ready to leave."

I turned to my new friend and said I had to leave because my father was calling.

Astonished, the wide-eyed little boy replied, "You're a kid?"

SENIOR PUNS

If old age is catching up with you...

walk faster.

If I own a ranch in my old age, I'm going to call it...

Pasture Prime.

I asked a hen the age-old question, what came first: the chicken or the egg?

The poor thing went through an eggsistential crisis.

"Grandpa, are your two horses brothers or just best friends?"

"They are not brothers, sweetheart, and I am not sure they are best friends, but one thing's for sure,

they are definitely neigh-bours."

I used to be a banker...

but then I lost interest.

Grandma had to get a tuberculosis test for work. I guess we'll finally have an answer to the age-old question...

TB or not TB?

If you lose something in a home for the elderly,

don't stop looking until you've searched every nook...

and granny.

I heard that old-time hockey players get...

gerihat-tricks.

I was a pastry chef once.

I quit because I realized that...

old age crepes up on you.

❖

The retirement home was very secure.

Each door was guarded by a century.

❖

A 100-year-old woman says her secret to old age is walking around barefoot and never brushing her teeth.

She's a super calloused fragile mistress hexed with halitosis.

❖

This girl said she recognized me from the vegetarian club but...

I'd never met herbivore.

Stars are like false teeth.

They come out at night.

When I was young,

I got a job at a bakery.

I kneaded the dough.

The only thing I ever won for aging was...

atrophy.

❖

My age defies gravity. It goes up...

and never comes down.

❖

Ozzy Osbourne was giving an elderly woman a piggyback, but then he dropped her.

The old lady was off her rocker.

❖

I started out with nothing...
and I still have most of it.

I heard when chemists die...
they barium.

I didn't like my beard at first...
then it grew on me.

Don't worry about old age.
It doesn't last.

An elderly man had some landscapers take care of his lawn every weekend for several years.

One day, he hired a new crew but forgot to fire the old one. The next weekend, they both showed up to mow his lawn and got into a fight over who should be there.

He had no idea he had started a turf war.

❖

I did a good deed today by giving up my seat on the bus to an elderly lady.

How was I supposed to know she'd never driven a bus before?

❖

I just named an elderly rabbit.

Harold *seemed appropriate.*

An older Italian man was teaching others how to use herbs in their cooking.

He gave sage advice.

You know that elderly male relative who's always taking pictures?

He's Papa Razzi.

The most dangerous season for elderly
people is...

   fall.

An elderly woman at the bank today
told me to check her balance.

   I pushed her over.

I'm working for a charity that provides
support for elderly grapes.

   My job is in raisin awareness.

An elderly couple from Russia was walking in St. Petersburg Square one cold evening, when a light precipitation began to fall.

"It looks like rain," said the man.

"Oh no, dear; it's definitely snow. Look at the way it blows in the light," said the woman.

The man turned to his wife and said,

"Let's ask the military officer over there. Hey, Officer Rudolph, is it raining or snowing?"

"Definitely raining, sir!" he replied.

"See, Rudolph the Red knows rain, dear!"

❖

Those elderly people with really good hearing are...

deaf defying.

What is the elderly's favorite genre of music?

Hip-pop.

A short nap once in a while can prevent old age...

especially while driving.

You know that elderly man who is always shouting?

That's Old Yeller.

Pixar decided on a name for their movie about an elderly man who attached balloons to his house.

They made it Up.

In the old days, excessive use of commas was considered a serious crime.

It usually resulted in a long sentence.

Every time Grandma makes venison for dinner, Grandpa says...

"Oh, deer!"

Isn't a limerick said by an elderly pirate...

the rhyme of the ancient mariner?

My dad and I were watching two older men play chess in the park, but they were speaking a foreign language. After a few minutes of silently watching them, I finally asked, "Is that Russian?"

"No," Dad replied, "it's Czech, Mate."

They say that married women grow appendages from their tailbone when they become elderly...

but that's just an old wives' tail.

I'm sick of all these elderly jokes.

They're getting old.

The retirement center where my grandmother lives has an annual 4th-of-July ball for the residents.

It's called "In Depends Dance Day."

My dad just retired and has taken up tinkering around with antique clocks.

He says they help pass the time.

My grandfather decided to enter a kickboxing tournament. He wasn't athletic, and he'd never fought before. We thought he was crazy to even enter it, but he said he had a plan to win; he would wrap his feet in underwear.

We didn't see how that would help, but he surprised us all and went...

undie-feeted.

The time period from 476-800 AD is known as the Dark Ages.

I guess that's because it was the time of knights.

Aging is hard. When I saw my first gray hair...

I felt like dyeing.

A friend of mine went bald years ago, but he still carries around an old comb.

He just can't part with it.

Yesterday, I ran into the man who once sold me an antique globe.

It's a small world.

I think my wife is putting glue on my antique weapons collection.

Of course, she denies it, but I'm sticking to my guns.

The time period between the Bronze and Iron Ages, where humans learned to cure meat, was called...

the Sausages.

Where did Noah keep his old bees?

In the Ark Hive.

❖

As I handed my Dad his fiftieth birthday card, he looked at me with tears in his eyes and said,

"You know, one would have been enough."

❖

If all is not lost...

where is it?

❖

It's not hard to meet expenses.

They're everywhere.

❖

Funny, I don't remember being...

absent minded.

❖

I wish the buck stopped here.

I sure could use a few.

❖

It's hard to make a comeback...

when you haven't been anywhere.

❖

I finally finished shooting my documentary about antique clocks.

It's about time.

Women should not have babies after forty.

That's too many babies.

These days, I spend a lot of time thinking about the hereafter.

I go somewhere to get something...

and then wonder what I'm hereafter.

THE BENEFITS

People no longer view you as a hypochondriac.

You don't have gray hair. They are wisdom highlights.

You just happen to be very wise.

63

Old age isn't so bad when you consider
the alternative.

❖

When you lose your memory,

you meet new friends every day.

❖

You get into heated arguments about
pension plans.

❖

When you lose your glasses, they're
usually close by.

Like on your forehead.

❖

You're not getting older;

you're becoming a classic!

❖

You enjoy hearing about other people's operations.

❖

Your secrets are safe with your friends because they can't remember them either.

❖

There is nothing left to learn the hard way.

❖

Your eyes won't get much worse.

You have the senility to forget the people you never liked,

the good fortune to run into the ones you do,

and the eyesight to tell the difference.

Your joints are more accurate meteorologists than the national weather service.

Your supply of brain cells is finally down to manageable size.

❖

Things you buy now won't wear out.

❖

You can eat dinner at 4 pm.

❖

You no longer think of speed limits as a challenge.

❖

You sing along with elevator music.

REMEMBER WHEN...?

All the girls had ugly gym uniforms?

❖

Nobody owned a purebred dog?

❖

A quarter was a decent allowance?

❖

It took five minutes for the TV
to warm up?

❖

Nearly everyone's Mom was at home
when the kids got home from school?

❖

Your Mom wore nylons that came in
two pieces?

❖

All your male teachers wore ties and
female teachers had their hair done
every day and wore high heels?

❖

You got your windshield cleaned, oil checked, and gas pumped, without asking, all for free, every time?

❖

You didn't pay for air, and you got trading stamps to boot?

❖

Laundry detergent had free glasses, dishes, or towels hidden inside the box?

❖

It was considered a great privilege to be taken out to dinner at a real restaurant with your parents?

❖

You'd reach into a muddy gutter
for a penny?

❖

They threatened to keep kids back a
grade if they failed, and they did?

❖

A 57 Chevy was everyone's dream car
for cruising, peeling out, laying rubber,
or watching drive-in movies?

❖

No one ever asked where the car keys
were because they were always in the
car, in the ignition, and the doors were
never locked?

❖

You could lie on your back in the grass with your friends and say things like, "That cloud looks like a..."?

❖

You played baseball with no adults to help kids with the rules of the game?

❖

Stuff from the store came without safety caps and seals because no one had yet tried to poison a perfect stranger?

❖

Being sent to the principal's office was nothing compared to the fate that awaited you at home?

❖

Everyone knew who Nancy Drew, the Hardy Boys, Laurel and Hardy, Howdy Doody and the Peanut Gallery, the Lone Ranger, Nellie Bell, Roy and Dale, and Trigger and Buttermilk were?

❖

The corner store sold ice cream for a nickel or a dime and sherbet in a squeeze cup for two or four cents?

❖

You feared for your life not because of drive-by shootings, drugs, or gangs, but because your parents and grandparents were a much bigger threat?

❖

Summers were filled with bike rides, baseball games, Hula Hoops, bowling, visits to the pool, and eating Kool-Aid powder with sugar?

❖

You smoked candy cigarettes?

❖

Coffee shops had tableside jukeboxes?

❖

You ate wax Coke-shaped bottles with colored sugar water filling?

❖

Pop machines dispensed glass bottles?

❖

Milk was delivered to your house in glass bottles with cardboard stoppers?

❖

There were newsreels before the movie, and an intermission in the middle?

❖

Ice cube trays were made of metal and had levers?

❖

The coolest toys were cork pop guns, TinkerToys, Erector Sets, Lincoln Logs, peashooters, roller skates, and P.F. Fliers?

❖

Hamburgers from McDonalds were fifteen cents?

❖

It wasn't odd to have two or three "best" friends?

❖

Baseball cards came in five-cent packs with a slab of bubblegum?

❖

Catching fireflies could happily occupy an entire evening?

❖

Gas was thirty-five cents a gallon?

❖

Party lines, mimeograph paper, Studebakers, washtub wringers, Reel-To-Reel tape recorders, penny candy, and Jiffy Pop popcorn were a thing?

❖

A foot of snow was a dream come true?

"Oly-oly-oxen-free" made perfect sense?

Spinning around, getting dizzy, and falling down was cause for giggles?

War was a card game?

Baseball cards in the spokes transformed any bike into a motorcycle?

❖

Taking drugs meant eating orange-flavored chewable aspirin?

❖

Fast food was what you ate during Lent?

❖

Time sharing meant togetherness, not computers or condominiums?

❖

A chip was a piece of wood; hardware was hardware, and software wasn't even a word?

Having a meaningful relationship meant getting along well with your cousins?

There were five-and-dime stores where you actually bought things for five or ten cents?

You could ride a street car, make a phone call, buy a Pepsi, or purchase enough stamps to mail one letter and two postcards for a nickel?

❖

Cigarette smoking was fashionable?

❖

You could buy a new Chevy coupe for $500, but no one could afford one?

❖

Water balloons were the ultimate weapon?

YOU KNOW YOU'RE OLD WHEN...

Instead of the John, you call your bathroom the Jim.

It sounds better when you say you go to the Jim first thing every morning.

You have a party...

and the neighbors don't even realize it.

You see an old person...

and realize you went to school together.

You take a nap...

to get ready for bed.

Your head makes dates...

your body can't keep.

You lean over to pick something up off the floor and ask yourself...

"Is there anything else I need to do while I'm down here?"

You use valet parking...

    to avoid losing your car.

Everything hurts and what doesn't hurt...

    doesn't work.

The gleam in your eyes...

    is from the sun hitting your bifocals.

Your little black book contains...

    only names that end in M.D.

Your children begin to look...

    middle aged.

You finally reach the top of the ladder...

and find it leaning against the wrong wall.

You look forward to...

a dull evening.

Your favorite part of the newspaper is...

20 Years Ago Today.

You turn out the lights for...

economic not romantic reasons.

You sit in a rocking chair...

and can't get it going.

Your knees buckle...

but your belt won't.

Your back goes out...

more than you do.

The little old gray-haired lady you
helped across the street...

is your wife.

You sink your teeth into a steak...

and they stay there.

You walk around mostly wondering...

what you're forgetting.

You have too much room in the house...

and not enough in the medicine
cabinet.

You know all the answers...

but nobody asks you the questions.

You're asleep...

but others worry that you're dead.

You're the life of the party...

if it lasts until eight o'clock.

Your memory is shorter...

and your complaining lasts longer.

Your wild oats have turned into...

prunes and All Bran.

You quit trying to hold your
stomach in...

no matter who walks into the room.

You wake up looking like...

your driver's license picture.

You're very good at telling stories...

over and over and over and over.

All you want for your birthday is...

to not be reminded of your age.

You're interested in going home...

*before you get to where you
are going.*

You're awake many hours...

*before your body allows you
to get up.*

You're very good at opening
childproof caps...

with a hammer.

You smile all the time...

*because you can't hear a thing
anyone is saying.*

You're aware that other people's great grandchildren...

are not nearly as cute as yours.

You feel cared for...

long term care, eye care, private care, dental care.

You are not really grouchy; you just don't like...

traffic, waiting, crowds, lawyers, loud music, unruly kids, commercials, barking dogs, politicians, and a few other things you can't seem to remember right now.

You're on vacation and your energy runs out...

before your money does.

You are sure everything you can't find is...

in a safe, secure place somewhere.

You wonder how your kids can be...

older than you feel.

Your idea of a night out...

is sitting on the patio.

You think they are making adults much younger these days.

When did they let kids become police officers, teachers, and doctors?

You have trouble remembering simple words like...

???

You're wrinkled, saggy, lumpy...

and that's just your left leg.

You feel like a walking storeroom of facts...

but you've lost the key to the storeroom door.

You and your teeth...

don't sleep together.

You try to straighten out the wrinkles in your socks...

and discover you aren't wearing any.

At the breakfast table you hear snap, crackle, pop...

and you're not eating cereal.

It takes two attempts...

to get up from the couch.

Happy hour is...

a nap.

You say something to your kids that your mother said to you...

and you always hated it.

You step off a curb and look down one more time...

to make sure the street is still there.

Your idea of weightlifting...

is standing up.

You thought you had more patience...

but it's really that you just don't care anymore.

It takes longer to rest...

than it did to get tired.

You give up all your bad habits...

and still don't feel good.

The pharmacist has become...

your new best friend.

You're finally holding all the cards...

and everyone decides to play chess.

It takes twice as long...

to look half as good.

You wonder how you could be
over the hill...

*when you don't even remember being
on top of it.*

You aren't afraid of monsters under
the bed anymore

because you know that if you get eaten
by one...

*you won't have to go to work the
next day.*

You've finally come to the
conclusion that...

life is officially unfair.